Earth
Then and Now

Robert Quinn

Contents

OXFORD
UNIVERSITY PRESS

UNIVERSITY PRESS

Great Clarendon Street, Oxford, OX2 6DP, United Kingdom

Oxford University Press is a department of the University of Oxford. It furthers the University's objective of excellence in research, scholarship, and education by publishing worldwide. Oxford is a registered trade mark of Oxford University Press in the UK and in certain other countries

© Oxford University Press 2011

The moral rights of the author have been asserted

First published in 2011

2015 2014 2013 2012 2011

10 9 8 7 6 5 4 3 2 1

ISBN: 978 0 19 464565 2

An Audio CD Pack containing this book and a CD is also available, ISBN 978 0 19 464605 5

The CD has a choice of American and British English recordings of the complete text.

An accompanying Activity Book is also available, ISBN 978 0 19 464575 1

Printed in China

This book is printed on paper from certified and well-managed sources.

ACKNOWLEDGEMENTS

Illustrations by: Kelly Kennedy pp.4, 26, 33; Ian Moores pp.5, 6, 8, 15, 16, 17, 19, 29, 30; Alan Rowe pp.38, 44.

The publisher would like to thank the following for their kind permission to reproduce photographs and other copyright material: Alamy Images pp.14 (Striated rock formation/ Harrison Smith), 20 (Spore capsules of moss/Bill Brookes), 20 (Limestone fern/FloralImages); Corbis pp.6 (Ash plume from the Eyjafjallajokull eruption/Arctic-Images), 12 (Stones/ Ocean), 14 (A trilobite/DK Limited), 23 (Meandering River in Tambopata Candamo National Reserve/Frans Lanting), 24 (A shoal with jellyfish/Martin Almqvist/Johnér Images); Getty Images pp.7 (Undersea volcano erupts/Dana Stephenson), 10 (Djibouti Lake Assal Area/Sean Gallup), 11 (Anhumas Abyss/SambaPhoto/Leonardo Papini), 19 (Sugata Valley, Kenya/Chris Johns/National Geographic), 21 (Ancient Bristlecone Pine/Curtis W. Richter/Photographer's Choice), 25 (Pygmy sweepers over coral reef/Georgette Douwman/ Photographer's Choice), 26 (Red-headed rock agama/ PhotoStock-Israel/Flickr), 35 (Furtwangler Glacier, Mount Kilimanjaro/Dori Moreno/Gallo Images); NASA pp.3 (Earth from space), 32 (Earth at night); Nature Picture Library p.27 (Camel with calf/Hanne & Jens Eriksen); Oxford University Press pp.8 (Waves/Photodisc), 12 (Amethyst geode/ Photodisc), 22 (Field of wild flowers/Design Pics), 28 (Glacier in Alaska/Photodisc); Photolibrary pp.9 (Stromatolites at Shark Bay/Ted Mead), 13 (Giants Causeway/DV/White), 17 (Mt. Aconcagua/FB-Fischer/Imagebroker), 18 (Stratified rock at Agio Pavlos/Marco Simoni/Robert Harding Travel), 22 (Fossil flower/Jack Clark/Animals Animals), 29 (Tracy Arm Fjord, Alaska/Sunset Avenue Productions/White), 31 (Flood/Barbara Boensch/Imagebroker), 33 (Pineapple fields/Dana Edmunds/ Pacific Stock), 34 (Smoke stacks/John Short/Design Pics Inc); Science Photo Library pp.4 (Planetary formation/Take 27 Ltd), 9 (Nostoc algae/Sinclair Stammers), 13 (Density of pumice and obsidian/Sheila Terry).

With thanks to Ann Fullick for science checking

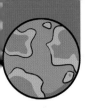

Introduction

Did you know that Earth formed billions of years ago? Our planet has changed a lot since then. The oceans and continents have moved. The plants and animals that we see today were not always here – some are old and some are new. People are new, too. Scientists say that we have only been here for about 200,000 years!

How did Earth form?
When did plants and animals first appear?
Where did the first people live on Earth?
How do oceans and continents move?
What keeps Earth warm?

Earth Today

Now read and discover more about Earth in the past and Earth today!

Scientists think that Earth is about 4.6 billion years old. Our planet started as an enormous ball of fire!

How Earth Formed

Scientists think that Earth formed from a cloud of gas, dust, and rock that was around our sun. These materials came together and formed a ball of fire and liquid rock. At that time, the temperature on Earth's surface was very hot, and nothing lived here.

Discover!

The Great Pyramid in Egypt is about 4,600 years old. Earth is one million times older than that!

4,600 YEARS OLD

Earth's Layers

After millions of years, Earth cooled down. The surface became a layer of solid rock, called the crust. This is the part of Earth that we live on. The crust is usually about 30 kilometers thick on land, but it's thinner at the bottom of the ocean.

Under Earth's crust, there's a layer called the mantle. It's about 2,900 kilometers thick. The mantle is very hot – its temperature is about 3,000 degrees centigrade. It's mostly made of liquid rock, called magma.

Earth's core is under the mantle, at the center of the planet. The core is about 3,500 kilometers across and it's mostly made of two metals – iron and nickel. The outer core is liquid, but the inner core is solid. That's because the other layers push down on the inner core with incredible pressure. Temperatures in the inner core can be more than 6,000 degrees centigrade.

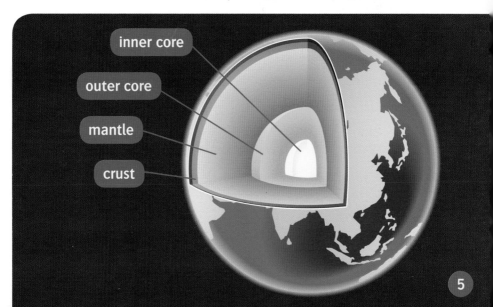

inner core

outer core

mantle

crust

gas and ash

vent

lava

cone

magma chamber

A Volcano Erupting

Mountains of Fire

There's a lot of heat in Earth's core and mantle. We can see some of this heat when volcanoes erupt and produce lava. In some parts of Earth's crust, magma forms underground pools, called magma chambers. When there's a lot of magma in a chamber, the magma moves up a tunnel to the surface. When the magma gets to Earth's surface, it's called lava. The lava comes out of holes called vents. Some volcanoes also produce lots of gas and ash. The lava and the ash can sometimes form a tall cone.

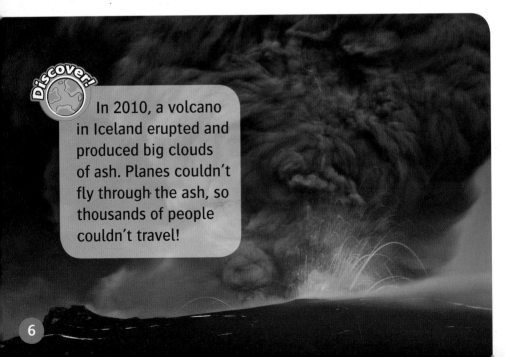

Discover!

In 2010, a volcano in Iceland erupted and produced big clouds of ash. Planes couldn't fly through the ash, so thousands of people couldn't travel!

Underwater Volcanoes

Sometimes volcanic vents form under the ocean. When this happens, the lava cools very quickly and makes round shapes, called pillow lava. Underwater lava can also build up and form volcanic islands, like Iceland or Hawaii. One of the newest volcanic islands on our planet is Hunga Ha'apai, near Tonga in the Pacific Ocean. This island appeared after a big underwater eruption in 2009.

An Underwater Eruption Near Tonga

Go to pages 36–37 for activities.

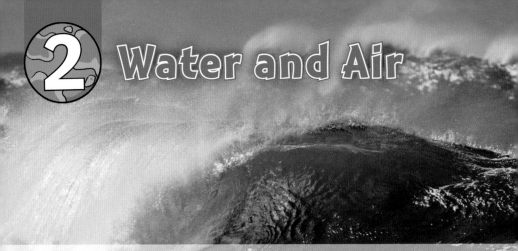

Today, water covers about 70% of our planet. Billions of years ago, Earth's surface was dry, and nothing lived here. Earth's atmosphere was also different. It had lots of carbon dioxide and other gases, but no oxygen.

How the Oceans Formed

At first, there wasn't any liquid water on Earth's surface, but there was lots of water vapor in the atmosphere. This water vapor came from inside the planet when volcanoes erupted. When Earth cooled down, the water vapor condensed and formed clouds in the sky. Then it started to rain. After millions of years, liquid water covered most of our planet's surface!

Discover!

Some of our planet's water came from millions of icy meteorites. When the meteorites entered Earth's atmosphere, the ice heated up and changed to water vapor.

Oxygen

About 3 billion years ago, something amazing happened – living things appeared on Earth! Some of the first living things were tiny blue-green bacteria. These bacteria grew in shallow pools of warm water and we can find their fossils today. The fossils look like rocks with unusual shapes and they're called stromatolites.

Blue-green bacteria used sunlight, water, and carbon dioxide to make their own food, like plants do today. The blue-green bacteria also produced oxygen, and after millions of years, there was lots of oxygen in Earth's oceans and atmosphere. Today, the air that we breathe is about 21% oxygen. We couldn't live without it!

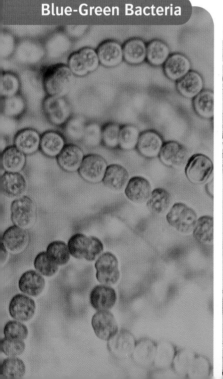

Blue-Green Bacteria

Stromatolite Fossils

Salt Water

Today, the water in our oceans and seas is about 3.5% salt. Do you know why? When rain falls on land, some of it goes into lakes and rivers, and then into the oceans. As the water moves, it picks up salt from the ground. When the water goes into the ocean, it carries this salt with it. After many millions of years, this has made our oceans salty.

Some lakes can be very salty, like Lake Assal in Djibouti in Africa. In this lake, the water is more than 35% salt, and no plants or animals can live there. The salt water comes from underground hot springs. When the hot water evaporates into the air, it leaves the salt in the lake.

Lake Assal, Djibouti

Fresh Water

Only 3% of Earth's water is fresh water. About 69% of this fresh water is frozen in polar ice, snow, and glaciers. About 30% is in underground caves and aquifers, between the rocks of Earth's crust. The other 1% is on the surface, in rivers and lakes.

One of the largest aquifers in the world is the Guaraní Aquifer, in South America. It covers about 1,200,000 square kilometers under Argentina, Brazil, Paraguay, and Uruguay. In this aquifer there are about 50,000 cubic kilometers of water. That's about two times the water in all the Great Lakes in North America!

Discover! Scientists say that there's enough water in the Guaraní Aquifer for everyone in the world to drink for 200 years.

→ Go to pages 38–39 for activities.

3 Minerals and Rock

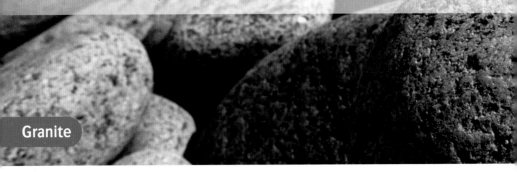

Earth's crust is solid rock that's made of minerals. There are three types of rock – igneous rock, sedimentary rock, and metamorphic rock. Do you know how they form?

Granite

Minerals

Rock is made of minerals that form crystals. Some types of rock, like granite, have small crystals. We can see their different colors. In other types of rock, like amethyst, the crystals are bigger and easier to see.

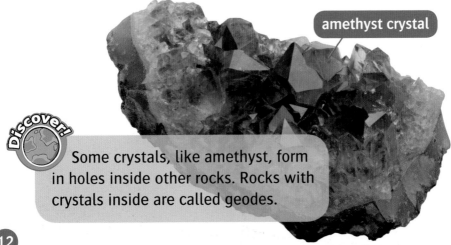

amethyst crystal

Discover!

Some crystals, like amethyst, form in holes inside other rocks. Rocks with crystals inside are called geodes.

Igneous Rock

Igneous rock forms when hot magma and lava cool down and become solid. Some examples are granite, pumice, and obsidian. Pumice is very light because it forms from lava that has lots of tiny air bubbles in it. Did you know that pumice can float on water? Obsidian is very different. It's heavy, volcanic rock, and it doesn't float.

pumice

obsidian

When igneous rock forms, it can create unusual shapes. The Giant's Causeway in Northern Ireland is an example. It formed during volcanic eruptions more than 60 million years ago. When the lava cooled down, it became a type of igneous rock called basalt. Then the basalt broke into about 40,000 tall columns. Now they look like giant stairs!

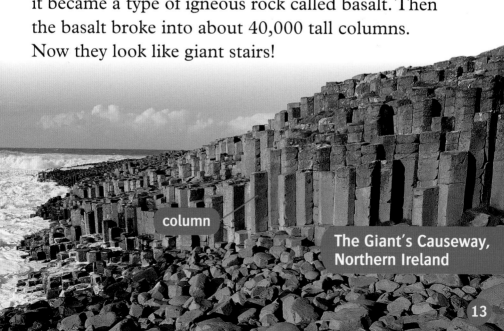

column

The Giant's Causeway, Northern Ireland

Sandstone Layers

Sedimentary Rock

Sedimentary rock is made of sediment – tiny pieces of rock, sand, and other materials. This sediment often forms layers at the bottom of rivers, lakes, and oceans. When there's a lot of sediment, the top layers push down on the bottom layers. This pressure slowly changes the sediment into solid rock. For example, limestone, sandstone, and shale form in this way. Sedimentary rock is interesting because it can tell us about Earth's past. Scientists often find fossils of dead plants and animals between the different layers of sediment.

Discover!

One of the best places for finding fossils is the Burgess Shale fossil field in Canada. Some of the fossils are more than 500 million years old.

Metamorphic Rock

Metamorphic rock is sedimentary rock or igneous rock that has changed because of lots of heat and pressure. This happens deep inside Earth, where there's heat from magma and lots of pressure from the rock above. For example, limestone changes into marble that's good for making statues. Shale changes into slate that's good for making roof tiles. Granite changes into a very hard rock called gneiss that's good for making buildings.

The Rock Cycle

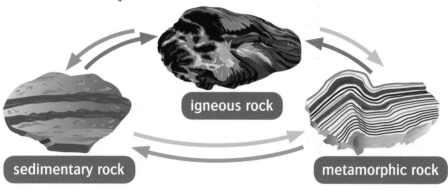

igneous rock

sedimentary rock

metamorphic rock

Rock can change in different ways. Sedimentary rock and igneous rock can change into metamorphic rock when there's lots of heat and pressure.

Metamorphic rock and sedimentary rock can melt and become magma. Then the magma cools down and becomes igneous rock.

Water and wind can cause erosion – they break igneous rock and metamorphic rock into tiny pieces. Then these pieces form new layers of sedimentary rock.

→ Go to pages 40–41 for activities.

4 Tectonic Plates

About 1.1 billion years ago, most of the land on Earth formed a giant continent called Rodinia. Today, the land is divided into smaller continents, with seas and oceans between them. How did this happen?

Moving Plates

Earth's crust is divided into enormous pieces, called tectonic plates. These plates fit together like a puzzle and they float on the magma in Earth's mantle. Tectonic plates also move around – about 10 centimeters every year. That doesn't sound like much, but in a million years a tectonic plate can move about 100 kilometers! That's how Rodinia changed to form the continents that we know today.

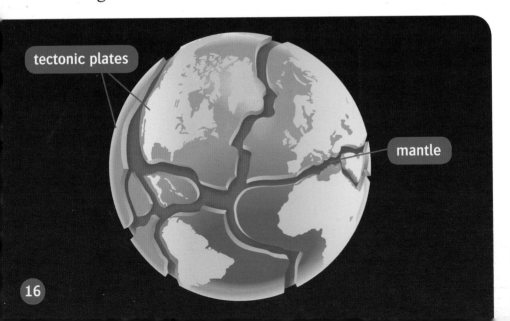

tectonic plates

mantle

When Tectonic Plates Meet

Some tectonic plates meet and then push together. One plate can push the other plate down into Earth's mantle, where it melts and changes into magma.

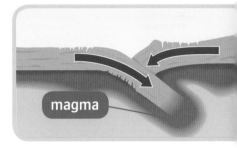

Sometimes two tectonic plates meet and push each other up to create new mountains. This is how the Andes Mountains formed in South America. The Andes Mountains are quite new – they're only about 76 million years old!

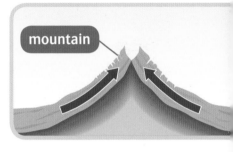

The highest mountain in the Andes is Mount Aconcagua in Argentina. It's 6,962 meters high.

Folded Rock

Folds and Rifts

Did you know that Earth's crust can bend and fold? This happens when tectonic plates push together very slowly, and for a very long time. We sometimes see these folds in the sides of hills and mountains.

When tectonic plates push together too hard or too quickly, they break into large blocks of rock that can move up, down, or to the side. Sometimes tectonic plates also move away from each other and make a long opening, called a rift.

When Earth's crust moves or breaks very suddenly, it can cause earthquakes. If an earthquake happens underwater, it can make a giant wave, called a tsunami.

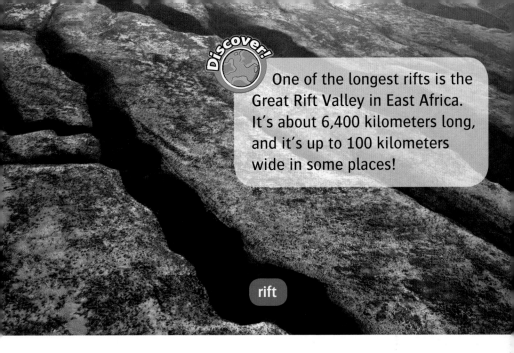

One of the longest rifts is the Great Rift Valley in East Africa. It's about 6,400 kilometers long, and it's up to 100 kilometers wide in some places!

rift

Ocean Rifts

Rift valleys can form at the bottom of Earth's oceans. When this happens, magma escapes from Earth's mantle and new crust forms on both sides of the rift. The new crust also pushes older crust to the sides. This is how tectonic plates grow bigger and move around.

Mountains can also form along rifts under oceans. For example, the Mid-Atlantic Rift goes down the middle of the Atlantic Ocean, from the Arctic to Antarctica. It's about 10,000 kilometers long. There are many underwater mountains on both sides of the rift.

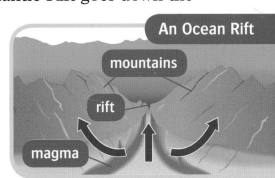

An Ocean Rift

mountains

rift

magma

→ Go to pages 42–43 for activities.

5 Plant Life

The first plants on Earth lived in the ocean. Then, plants started growing on land, too. Today, scientists have named more than 300,000 different species of plants around the world, and they are discovering more species every year!

The First Land Plants

The first land plants appeared more than 450 million years ago. They were non-seed plants, like mosses, that grew in cool places near water. These plants didn't have leaves and they didn't produce seeds. They reproduced by growing spore capsules with lots of tiny spores inside.

More than 300 million years ago, the first ferns appeared. They had long leaves called fronds with spore capsules on them. Today, there are more than 12,000 types of fern around the world.

Moss

spore capsules

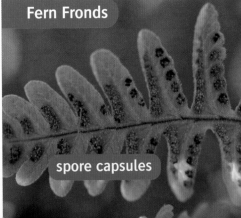

Fern Fronds

spore capsules

Seeds and Cones

Earth's first seed plants were conifers that appeared about 290 million years ago. These new plants grew their seeds inside cones to keep them safe. They also had tall trunks, long branches, and lots of thin needles. Soon, conifers started growing in many parts of the world. They were taller than ferns, so they got more sunlight.

A Bristlecone Pine Tree

Discover!

The oldest and tallest living things on Earth today are conifers – some bristlecone pine trees are more than 4,500 years old, and some redwood trees are more than 100 meters tall!

Flowering Plants

About 140 million years ago, the first flowering plants appeared. These plants didn't reproduce by growing cones – they produced flowers. First the wind and insects pollinated the flowers, and the flowers became fruit, with seeds inside. Then animals ate the fruit and carried the seeds to new places. Finally, new plants grew from those seeds.

Today, about 80% of the plants on Earth are flowering plants. Some of these plants give us food, like rice, vegetables, and of course, fruit! Flowering plants also give us other products like cotton and rubber.

Discover! Scientists have found fossil flowers in very old rocks. Some of them are more than 180 million years old!

Forests

Today about 30% of Earth's surface is covered by forests. In cold climates, most of the trees are conifers that stay green all year long. In warmer climates, there are deciduous trees that grow new leaves in spring. Then they lose the leaves in fall. In hot climates, there are often tropical rainforests, with many different types of plants.

In rainforests, the tallest trees form the canopy at the top, where there's lots of sunlight. Under the canopy, there are younger trees and lots of smaller plants like ferns and mosses. Rainforests are very important because the plants there produce lots of oxygen. Scientists can also make medicines from many plants that grow in rainforests.

Discover!

The biggest tropical rainforest is the Amazon Rainforest in South America.

→ Go to pages 44–45 for activities.

6 Animal Life

The first animals appeared in the ocean more than 700 million years ago. They were very simple living things, like comb jellies. All the animals that we see today, in water and on land, evolved from these ocean animals.

Comb Jellies

Early Invertebrates

For many millions of years, the only animals on Earth were invertebrates – animals with no backbone. Some of them had a hard cover or a shell that protected them. There are many types of invertebrate on Earth today. Some of them, like crabs and jellyfish, live in water. Others, like insects, live on land.

Discover!

In the Cambrian Period, about 540 million years ago, many new animals appeared in Earth's oceans. Scientists call this the Cambrian Explosion.

Fish and Amphibians

The first fish appeared about 510 million years ago. They were Earth's first vertebrates – animals with a backbone. Today there are about 24,000 different types of fish. All of them have gills to take oxygen from water. Most of them also have fins and a tail to help them to swim.

Scientists think that amphibians evolved from fish that lived in shallow water. About 400 million years ago, amphibians became the first vertebrates that lived on land and walked on legs. Young amphibians have gills, but then they grow lungs so that they can breathe air. There are more than 4,000 species of amphibian today, like frogs, toads, and salamanders.

Ocean Fish

A Lizard

Reptiles and Birds

Reptiles are different from amphibians because they can stay on land all the time. They have scales to protect their skin, so that it doesn't get dry. Reptiles first appeared about 320 million years ago. They probably looked like small lizards. The most famous reptiles in history are the dinosaurs. They lived on Earth for about 150 million years, before they became extinct. Today, we can see many types of reptiles, like crocodiles, snakes, lizards, and turtles.

Some scientists believe that the first birds evolved from reptiles. There are fossils of dinosaurs, like microraptors, that had feathers! Today, there are many types of bird and most of them can fly. Some birds, like penguins and ostriches, have wings, but they can't fly.

Discover!

One of the first birds was the Archaeopteryx. It lived about 150 million years ago.

A Camel Feeding Her Baby

Mammals

Mammals are the only animals that give birth to their young. They don't lay eggs, like fish, amphibians, reptiles, or birds do. Mammal mothers are special because they produce milk for their babies to drink.

Scientists think that early mammals evolved from small reptiles, like lizards, about 250 million years ago. When the dinosaurs became extinct, more mammals appeared. Later, mammals also became larger and more intelligent.

Today, we can find many different types of mammal. Some live on land, like horses, camels, and monkeys. Others live in the ocean, like whales and dolphins. Bats are special because they are the only mammals that can fly. Did you know that you are a mammal, too?

→ Go to pages 46–47 for activities.

27

glacier

Earth's temperature has changed many times in the past. There have been very cold times, when large areas of land were covered with ice. There have also been times when Earth's climate was very warm and tropical.

Ice Ages

During ice ages, Earth's temperature is very cold for a long time. Winters become colder and longer, and large glaciers form, especially at Earth's Poles. This happens because the Poles get less sunlight than other places on Earth. Glaciers reflect lots of sunlight into space, which makes Earth's temperature much colder. The last ice age ended more than 10,000 years ago.

Glaciers

Glaciers form slowly, but they can become very big. The world's largest glacier is the Lambert Glacier in Antarctica. It's about 500 kilometers long, 80 kilometers wide, and 2.5 kilometers deep! This glacier moves about 600 meters every year.

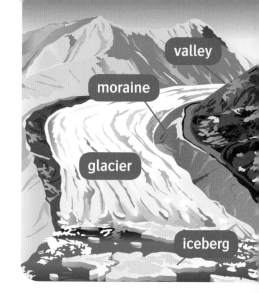

When glaciers move, they cut long valleys, called glacial valleys, in the ground. Glaciers carry materials like rocks and soil with them. When glaciers melt and disappear, these materials form long hills, called moraines.

Some glacial valleys form on coasts. The ice moves down to the ocean and big pieces fall into the water. This is how many icebergs form. When the ocean fills a glacial valley, it's called a fjord.

A Fjord in Alaska

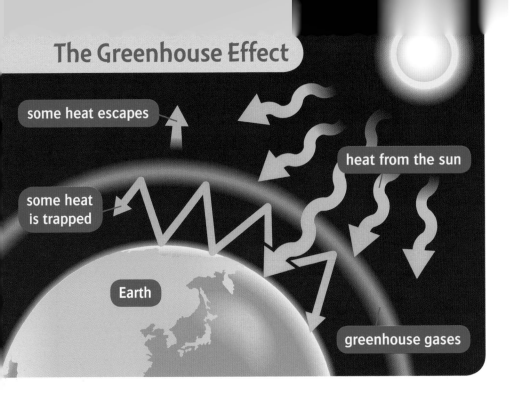

The Greenhouse Effect

some heat escapes

heat from the sun

some heat is trapped

Earth

greenhouse gases

Earth gets heat from the sun. Some of this heat escapes into space, and some is trapped by gases, like carbon dioxide and methane. This is called the greenhouse effect because it works like a greenhouse. The greenhouse effect is important because it keeps Earth warm enough for us to live here.

Greenhouse Periods

Very warm periods in Earth's history are called greenhouse periods. Plants grow very well during greenhouse periods because it's warm and there's more carbon dioxide for plants to make their food. During some greenhouse periods in the past, there were tropical plants in Antarctica!

Floods

During greenhouse periods, glaciers start to melt and they get smaller, so they can't reflect a lot of sunlight back into space. This makes Earth's temperature warmer. The water that comes from glaciers makes sea levels go up, and this can cause floods along coasts.

The land gets warmer during greenhouse periods, too. In the Arctic, there's a lot of methane in the frozen soil. When the soil gets warmer, methane comes out of the soil and goes into the atmosphere. This increases the greenhouse effect, and Earth gets warmer more quickly.

→ Go to pages 48–49 for activities.

8 People on Earth

About 200,000 years ago, early people only lived in Africa. Today, almost seven billion people live all over Earth! People have changed our planet in many ways.

What Have People Changed?

Some places on Earth haven't changed very much. They are natural areas, like rainforests and national parks. Natural areas are important because they are homes for many plants and animals. We need to care for these areas so that plants and animals can live there in the future.

In other areas, people have changed many things. In rural areas, farmers have cut down trees and they have cleared land to grow crops for people to eat. In urban areas, like towns and cities, people have built lots of homes and other buildings. They have also built roads, bridges, and tunnels.

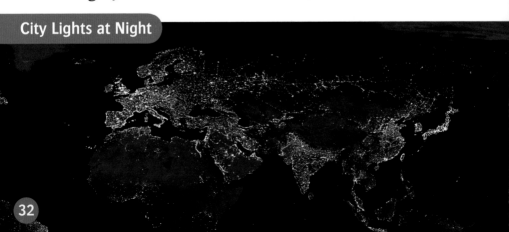

City Lights at Night

Natural Resources

Earth gives us lots of resources like food and other products from plants and animals. It also gives us water to drink and air to breathe. These natural resources are renewable – they replace themselves naturally. We can get more of these resources, but we need to share them with other people. In some parts of the world, people don't have enough food or enough clean water.

Earth also gives us mineral resources, like metals, that we use to make products in factories. We burn fossil fuels, like oil, coal, and gas, to produce energy. These resources are non-renewable. We can't get any more, so we need to use them carefully.

Discover!

We can get renewable energy from the sun, the wind, and moving water.

33

Waste and Pollution

We throw away too much waste, and this is bad for our planet. We need to reduce the amount of waste that we produce – we can recycle more things, like paper, plastic, glass, and metal.

Our cars and factories produce smoke that pollutes the air. In some cities, it can be difficult to breathe because there's so much pollution in the air. Some factories pollute our water and soil. We should build more modern factories that don't produce so much pollution.

Pollution from Factories

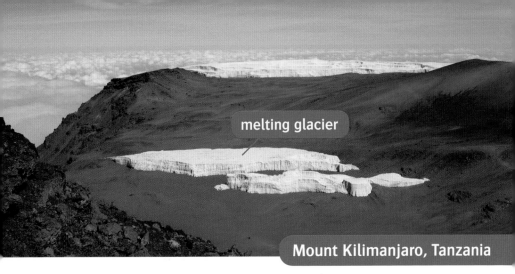

melting glacier

Mount Kilimanjaro, Tanzania

Global Warming

Scientists think that a new greenhouse period is starting. Earth is getting warmer, and many glaciers are melting, like the ones on Mount Kilimanjaro in Tanzania. Why is this happening? For the last 150 years, people have burned lots of fossil fuels, and this makes gases like carbon dioxide. The carbon dioxide is increasing the natural greenhouse effect, and making Earth warmer. This is called global warming.

We need to produce less carbon dioxide. We also need to protect our forests and plant new trees. Trees use carbon dioxide and slow down global warming.

Caring for Our Planet

We live on a beautiful planet that has been here for billions of years. Earth gives us everything that we need to live. Now we need to care for our planet so that our children and our grandchildren can enjoy it in the future, too!

→ Go to pages 50–51 for activities.

1 A Ball of Fire

← Read pages 4–7.

1 Complete the sentences.

core   crust   fire   ~~gas~~   iron   mantle

1 Earth formed from a cloud of _____gas_____ , dust,
and rock.

2 Earth started as a hot ball of _____ and liquid rock.

3 Earth's surface is a layer of solid rock called the

_____ .

4 Earth's _____ is mostly liquid rock called magma.

5 Earth's _____ is about 3,500 kilometers across.

6 Earth's core is made of _____ and nickel.

2 Write *true* or *false*.

1 Earth is about 4.6 million years old.   _false_

2 We are living on Earth's crust.   _____

3 The mantle is about 2,900 kilometers thick.   _____

4 The core is about 1,300 kilometers across.   _____

5 Magma chambers form in the Earth's core.   _____

6 Lava is magma that gets to Earth's surface.   _____

7 In 2010, a volcano in Iceland erupted.   _____

8 Hunga Ha'apai is one of the oldest volcanic islands.   _____

3 **Match. Then write the sentences.**

Magma forms	gets to Earth's surface.
The magma moves up	lots of gas and ash.
Lava is magma that	a tunnel to the surface.
The lava comes out of	a magma chamber.
Some volcanoes produce	at the top of some volcanoes.
There's a cone	a hole called a vent.

1 _Magma forms a magma chamber._

2 _____

3 _____

4 _____

5 _____

6 _____

4 **Answer the questions.**

1 What is the temperature of Earth's inner core?

It's about 6,000 degrees centigrade.

2 Where is Earth's crust the thickest?

_____

3 What shape is pillow lava?

_____

4 When did the island of Hunga Ha'apai form?

_____

5 How thick is Earth's crust on land?

_____

2 Water and Air

← Read pages 8–11.

river ~~cloud~~ glacier rain
lake atmosphere sky ocean

1 Write the words.

 1 _cloud_

 5 _____

 2 _____

 6 _____

 3 _____

 7 _____

 4 _____

 8 _____

2 Complete the sentences.

bacteria   food   meteorites   atmosphere   salt   vapor

1 At first, there wasn't any oxygen in Earth's _____.

2 Lots of water _____ came from inside the planet.

3 Some of Earth's water came from icy _____.

4 Blue-green _____ grew in pools of warm water.

5 Plants today can make their own _____.

6 The water in our oceans is about 3.5% _____.

3 Find and write twelve adjectives.

1 dry
2 f
3 f
4 h
5 i
6 l
7 l
8 s

u	n	d	e	r	g	r	o	u	n	d
n	s	h	a	l	l	o	w	w	w	g
u	f	r	o	z	e	n	s	a	i	o
s	d	a	u	q	o	l	a	r	g	e
u	f	r	e	s	h	d	l	m	i	h
a	n	p	a	t	o	r	t	w	c	o
l	i	q	u	i	d	y	y	k	y	t

9 s
10 u
11 u
12 w

4 Answer the questions.

1 When did living things appear on Earth?

2 What do stromatolites look like?

3 How much of Earth's atmosphere today is oxygen?

4 Why don't any plants or animals live in Lake Assal?

5 How much of Earth's water is fresh water?

6 Where is most of Earth's fresh water?

③ Minerals and Rock

← Read pages 12–15.

1 Find the words and complete the chart.

slatepupumicersmarbleimeslimestoneansandstone
stobsidianergneissiteshalerygraniteston

Igneous Rock	_____	_____	_____
Sedimentary Rock	_____	_____	_____
Metamorphic Rock	slate	_____	_____

2 Circle the correct words.

1 Granite has (small) / large crystals with different colors.

2 Amethyst **minerals** / **crystals** form in holes inside other rocks.

3 **Obsidian** / **Pumice** is a very light rock.

4 We often find fossils in **igneous** / **sedimentary** rock.

5 **Marble** / **Slate** is good for making statues.

6 Heat and pressure can change granite into **gneiss** / **shale**.

7 Earth's crust is made of **geodes** / **minerals**.

8 The Giant's Causeway is in **Northern Ireland** / **Canada**.

3 Complete the sentences.

break   change   cools   form   melt

1 Sedimentary rock can _____ into metamorphic rock when there's lots of heat and pressure.

2 Metamorphic rock can _____ and become magma.

3 When the magma _____ down, it becomes igneous rock.

4 Water and wind can _____ rock into tiny pieces.

5 These pieces of rock _____ new layers of sedimentary rock.

4 Answer the questions.

1 How are amethyst crystals different from granite crystals?

_____

2 What rock can float on water?

_____

3 How old is the Giant's Causeway? What is it made of?

_____

4 What can people find in the Burgess Shale?

_____

5 What do people usually make from slate?

_____

4 Tectonic Plates

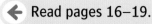 Read pages 16–19.

1 Match. Then write the sentences.

Earth's crust is divided	about 10 centimeters every year.
These plates float on	meet and then push together.
Tectonic plates move	two plates push each other up.
Some tectonic plates	the magma in Earth's mantle.
Mountains form when	into tectonic plates.

1 _____

2 _____

3 _____

4 _____

5 _____

2 Write *true* or *false*.

1 The Andes Mountains are 7 million years old. _____

2 The rock in Earth's crust can bend and fold. _____

3 Earthquakes can only happen on land. _____

4 A rift is a long opening between tectonic plates. _____

5 There are mountains under the Atlantic Ocean. _____

6 Tectonic plates can't become bigger or smaller. _____

3 Order the letters with the same color. Then write the words.

c	e	a	a	i	t
d	s	u	t	a	e
t	a	r	o	f	n
a	a	n	g	o	k
e	o	t	n	u	m
s	c	m	u	l	p
e	i	h	t	q	m
n	a	i	l	m	t

1 ☐ _____fold_____

2 ☐ _____

3 ☐ _____

4 ☐ _____

5 ☐ _____

6 ☐ _____

7 ☐ _____

4 Answer the questions.

1 How did Rodinia change to form smaller continents?

_____

2 How far can tectonic plates move in a million years?

_____

3 Where are the Andes Mountains? How old are they?

_____

4 How tall is Mount Aconcagua? Where is it?

_____

5 Where is the Great Rift Valley? How long is it?

_____

6 How long is the Mid-Atlantic Rift?

_____

43

5 Plant Life

← Read pages 20–23.

1 Write the words.

> cone   fern   flower   frond
> fruit   leaf   moss   needles
> seed   spore capsule

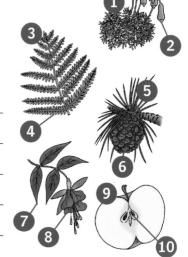

1 _____   6 _____

2 _____   7 _____

3 _____   8 _____

4 _____   9 _____

5 _____   10 _____

2 Complete the sentences.

> conifers   deciduous   flowering
> non-seed   spores   tropical

1 Mosses are one type of _____ plant.

2 Bristlecone pines and redwoods are _____.

3 Trees that grow new leaves every year are called

_____ trees.

4 Ferns reproduce by growing _____ on their fronds.

5 Some _____ plants produce fruit that we can eat.

6 Many different plants grow in _____ rainforests.

3 Correct the sentences.

1 Land plants appeared more than 600 million years ago.

Land plants appeared more than 450 million years ago.

2 Ferns have a trunk, with branches and thin needles.

3 Some redwood trees are more than 1,000 meters tall.

4 About 50% of the Earth is covered by forests.

5 Rainforests don't produce lots of oxygen.

4 Answer the questions.

1 How many species of plants have scientists named?

2 How tall are the tallest redwood trees?

3 When did the first flowering plants appear?

4 Where is the world's biggest rainforest today?

5 How many types of fern are there today?

6 Animal Life

← Read pages 24–27.

1 Write *true* or *false*.

1 Jellyfish are vertebrates. _____

2 Fish have lungs to take oxygen from water. _____

3 Frogs and salamanders are amphibians. _____

4 Dinosaurs lived on Earth for 320 million years. _____

5 Some types of dinosaur had feathers. _____

6 Mammal mothers lay eggs and produce milk. _____

2 Match. Then write the sentences.

Invertebrates	and a tail to help them to swim.
Most fish have fins	scales to protect their skin.
Penguins have wings,	mammals that can fly.
Amphibians were the	don't have a backbone.
Crocodiles have	first vertebrates on land.
Bats are the only	but they can't fly.

1 _____

2 _____

3 _____

4 _____

5 _____

6 _____

3 Order the letters and complete the puzzle.

1 rattevrebe

2 herfates

3 ltia

4 ibdr

5 nobabcke

6 lecsas

7 sulng

8 ehsil

9 sifn

10 lisgl

Crossword grid (1 down): v e r t e b r a t e

4 Answer the questions.

1 Where did Earth's first animals appear?

_____

2 How many types of fish are there today?

_____

3 What were the first vertebrates that lived on land?

_____

4 What did the first reptiles probably look like?

_____

5 What mammals live in the ocean?

_____

7 Temperature

← Read pages 28–31.

1 Circle the correct words.

1 Earth's temperature gets **hotter** / **colder** during an ice age.

2 Glaciers can become big, but they form very **slowly** / **quickly**.

3 Fjords form when the ocean fills a glacial **valley** / **lake**.

4 Greenhouse gases **reflect** / **trap** heat from sunlight.

5 Plants use **methane** / **carbon** dioxide to make their own food.

6 During greenhouse periods, glaciers get **larger** / **smaller**.

2 Complete the sentences.

hills   valleys   methane   plants   reflect   sunlight

1 The Poles get less _____ than other places
on Earth.

2 Glaciers _____ sunlight back into space.

3 In the past, there were tropical _____ in Antarctica.

4 There's a lot of _____ in the frozen soil in
the Arctic.

5 Moraines are long _____ that are made by glaciers.

6 When glaciers move, they cut long _____ in
the ground.

3 Order the words. Then write *true* or *false*.

1 changed. / temperature / Earth's / never / has

   Earth's temperature has never changed.   _false_

2 ice age / last / ago. / ended / The / 20,000 years

   _____   _____

3 Glacier / long. / is / Lambert / 80 kilometers / The

   _____   _____

4 effect / The / warm. / greenhouse / Earth / keeps

   _____   _____

5 up / levels / melt. / go / Sea / glaciers / when

   _____   _____

4 Answer the questions.

1 When do winters become colder and longer?

   _____

2 How deep is the ice in the Lambert Glacier?

   _____

3 What do glaciers carry with them?

   _____

4 Why is the greenhouse effect important for us?

   _____

5 Why do plants grow well during greenhouse periods?

   _____

8 People on Earth

← Read pages 32–35.

1 Complete the diagram.

natural   urban   rural

cities   crops   farms   towns
national parks   rainforests

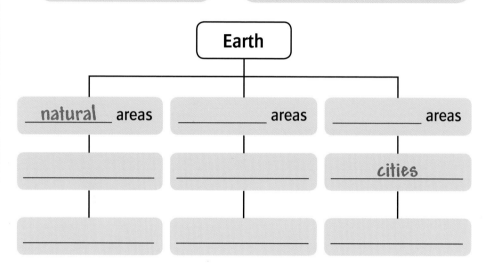

Earth

___natural___ areas   _____ areas   _____ areas

_____   _____   ___cities___

_____   _____   _____

2 Circle the odd one out. Then match.

1 plant, (pollution), animal

2 trees, buildings, bridges

3 coal, gas, water

4 carbon dioxide, oxygen, smoke

5 tunnels, mountains, oceans

It's a renewable resource.

They are made by people.

It's not a natural resource.

They are natural things.

It's a greenhouse gas.

3 **Answer the questions.**

1 Where did people live about 200,000 years ago?

_____

2 Why do we need to use non-renewable resouces carefully?

_____

3 What can we do to reduce the waste that we produce?

_____

4 Why are the glaciers on Mount Kilimanjaro melting?

_____

5 Why should we protect our forests?

_____

4 **Order the letters and write the words. Then complete the secret message.**

1 bnaru   1 ➤ | u | r | b | a | n |

2 romdne   2 ➤

3 aimlner   3 ➤

4 feublauti   4 ➤

5 weblernae   5 ➤

6 rualnta   6 ➤

7 lruar   7 ➤

The secret message is:

| C | | | | | f | | | | o | | | | p | | | | | |

1 Choose a national park in your country.

2 Complete the diagram with information about the park.

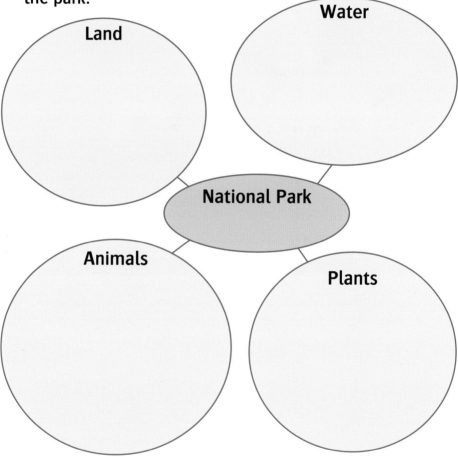

Land

Water

National Park

Animals

Plants

3 Make a poster about the national park. Write sentences and add pictures.

4 Display your poster.

An Earth Quiz

1 Write more true or false sentences about Earth's history.

Do the Earth Quiz!

Write *true* or *false*.

1 Earth is about 4.6 million years old.   _____

2 The Lambert Glacier is in Antarctica.   _____

3 _____   _____

4 _____   _____

5 _____   _____

6 _____   _____

7 _____   _____

8 _____   _____

9 _____   _____

10 _____   _____

11 _____   _____

12 _____   _____

2 Give the quiz to friends or people in your family.

3 Display your quiz and the results.

Glossary

appear to start to be seen

aquifer a layer of rock that can hold water

area a part of a place

atmosphere the gas and clouds around a planet

backbone the line of small bones down the middle of an animal's back

bacteria very simple living things

bend to become not straight

branch (*plural* **branches**) a part of a tree that grows out from the main part

breathe to take in and let out air through your nose and mouth

bubble a ball of gas

burn to make flames and heat

canopy the highest branches of the trees in a rainforest

carbon dioxide a gas in the air

carry to take something to another place

cause to make something happen

center the middle

climate the usual type of weather in a country

coal a hard, black fossil fuel

coast the land next to the sea or ocean

condense to change from gas into liquid

cone an object with a flat bottom and sides that make a triangular shape; the hard, dry fruit of a pine tree or a fir tree

conifer a tree that grows cones

cool down to become cooler

cover to put something over something; to be over something; a thing that's put over something

crab an ocean animal with a hard shell and eight legs

crop a plant that we grow in large amounts

cubic kilometer a space that's 1 kilometer long, 1 kilometer wide, 1 kilometer high

dead not living any more

deciduous trees that lose their leaves are deciduous

divide to break something into smaller parts

dust very small pieces of dirt

earthquake when the ground moves

energy we need energy to move and grow, and machines need energy to work

enormous very, very big

enough how much we want or need

erosion when water or wind breaks rock and soil into smaller pieces

erupt when a volcano erupts, it produces lava, ash, and gas

escape to get away from something

evaporate to change from liquid into gas

evolve to change very slowly and become something new

extinct when a species has died

feather birds have many of these; they are soft and light and cover their body

fin a thin part that sticks out from a fish's body and helps it to swim

fire this is produced when something burns; it's very hot

float to stay on the top of water

flood when there is a lot of water where it is usually dry

fold to bend so that one part lies on another part; where layers of rock fold

form to make or be made

fossil parts of dead plants or animals that have changed into rock

fresh not salty (for water)

fuel something that we use to produce heat or energy

gas not a solid or a liquid; like air

gill fish and some amphibians have these on the side of their head for breathing

give birth to to produce a baby or young animal

greenhouse a building made of glass for growing plants

hole a space in something

hot spring a place where hot water comes out of the ground

increase to get bigger; to make something bigger

inner on the inside

keep to stay; to make something stay

layer a flat piece of something

leaf (*plural* **leaves**) the flat part of a plant

liquid not a solid or a gas; like water

lung a part of the body that is for breathing; most animals and people have two

material something that we use to make other things

melt to become liquid because of being hot

metal a hard material made from minerals

meteorite a material from space that hits a planet

methane a type of gas

mineral a material that's in the ground

natural comes from nature; not made by people

needle something long and sharp; part of a conifer plant

non-renewable doesn't replace itself, so there isn't any more

oil a liquid fossil fuel from under the ground

outer on the outside

oxygen a gas that we need to breathe

pillow the soft thing that you put your head on in bed

planet a large, round thing in space that goes around a star

pollinate to put pollen into a flower or a plant so that it produces seeds

pollute to make air, land, or water dirty

pollution something that makes air, land, or water dirty

pressure the force or weight of something on another thing

produce to grow or make something

protect to keep safe from danger

push to make something move away

reduce to make something smaller or less

reflect to send back light

renewable replaces itself, so there is more

replace to put a new thing back in the place of an old one

reproduce to make more living things like oneself

resource something that we use to make or do things

roof tiles hard, flat things that cover the top of a house

rural in the countryside; not in the city

scale hard material that covers the skin of many fish and other animals

seed the small, hard part of a plant; a new plant can grow from this

shallow not deep

soil the ground that plants grow in

solid hard; not liquid or gas

space everything around Earth and outside Earth's atmosphere

spore tiny parts of mosses and ferns that grow into new plants

stairs parts of a building that we walk on to go up and down

statue a shape of a person or animal made of stone or metal

suddenly very quickly

sunlight light from the sun

surface the outside or the top of something

tail the part of an animal's body that comes out at the back

temperature how hot or cold something is

thick not thin

trap to keep something in a place where it can't escape

tropical from the Tropics

trunk the thick part of a tree

urban in towns or cities

valley the land between hills or mountains

waste things that we throw away

water vapor water when it is a gas

wave a line of water that moves across the top of the ocean

wing a part of a bird, insect, or bat's body; it's used for flying

without not having something; not doing something

young baby animals

Series Editor: Hazel Geatches • CLIL Adviser: John Clegg

Oxford Read and Discover graded readers are at four levels, from 3 to 6, suitable for students from age 8 and older. They cover many topics within three subject areas, and can support English across the curriculum, or Content and Language Integrated Learning (CLIL).

Available for each reader:
• Audio CD Pack (book & audio CD)
• Activity Book

For Teacher's Notes & CLIL Guidance go to
www.oup.com/elt/teacher/readanddiscover

Subject Area / Level	The World of Science & Technology	The Natural World	The World of Arts & Social Studies
3 600 headwords	• How We Make Products • Sound and Music • Super Structures • Your Five Senses	• Amazing Minibeasts • Animals in the Air • Life in Rainforests • Wonderful Water	• Festivals Around the World • Free Time Around the World
4 750 headwords	• All About Plants • How to Stay Healthy • Machines Then and Now • Why We Recycle	• All About Desert Life • All About Ocean Life • Animals at Night • Incredible Earth	• Animals in Art • Wonders of the Past
5 900 headwords	• Materials to Products • Medicine Then and Now • Transportation Then and Now • Wild Weather	• All About Islands • Animal Life Cycles • Exploring Our World • Great Migrations	• Homes Around the World • Our World in Art
6 1,050 headwords	• Cells and Microbes • Clothes Then and Now • Incredible Energy • Your Amazing Body	• All About Space • Caring for Our Planet • Earth Then and Now • Wonderful Ecosystems	• Helping Around the World • Food Around the World

For younger students, **Dolphin Readers** Levels Starter, 1, and 2 are available.